This Once-Only World

This Once-Only World

ADA JILL SCHNEIDER

PEARTREE PRESS: FALL RIVER, MASSACHUSETTS
2015

PearTree Press
P.O. Box 9585
Fall River, MA 02720
peartree-press.com

All rights reserved. No part of this book may be used or reproduced in any manner whatsoever scanned, or distributed in any printed or electronic form without written permission from the publisher, except in the case of brief quotations embodied in critical articles and reviews.

For information, write us at PearTree Press, P.O. Box 9585, Fall River, MA 02720.

LIBRARY OF CONGRESS CONTROL NUMBER: 2015934970

ISBN-13: 978-0-9908161-1-9

Printed in the United States of America on acid-free paper.

Book design by Stefani Koorey

Proofreading: Robert Schneider

Cover Photograph: "Entrada ao Cemitério Judaico em Horta, Faial" by Author

Photograph of Author: Brian Glantz

Copyright © 2015 by Ada Jill Schneider

Printed in the United States of America

1 3 5 7 9 10 8 6 4 2

*With unending love
for my children and grandchildren—*

*Marcy   Gregory   Erin
Gretchen   Lauren   Atlye
Lilly   Madison   Bryn*

—and always for my husband, Ron

CONTENTS

Reliance

Reliance	3
I Fit Into His Arms	4
I Scan Him Slowly	5
Spring, 1953	6
August, 1958	7
A Spoon and Fork	8
All That I Am	9
Happy 77th Birthday, My Love	10
Continuum	11
Understanding	12
Elasticity	13
Graffiti Me	14
Another Life	15
A Slow Lindy	16
Tango	17
Waltz	18
My Limbic Brain	19
Sir Christopher Wren's Garden	20
Pas de Deux	21
Cruise	22
Optional Tours for Married Couples	23

Working Class

Working Class	27
Privilege	28
Brooklyn, 1941	30
A Familiar Song	32
Mama Greenhorn	33
Leah	34
How Not to Buy a Dog	35
Best Wishes	36
Plagued	37
Round and Round We Go	38

Survey	39
Disorder	40
Hands Under the Table	41
75 Holds on to Railings	42
Ice Hockey	44
Once	45
I Saw It Coming	46
Time-Lapse	47
Inventory of Birds	48
You Can't Get Back In	49
Regrets?	50
Memory Manager	51
Tea Leaves	52
Advertisement	53

The Silence of Fireflies

Avian Victoriana	57
Spectrum	58
In the Beginning	59
Seven Little Goslings	60
Starring the River	61
To Hold a Hummingbird	62
Hummers on Guard	63
The Azores in May	64
The Sidewalks of Ponta Delgada	65
On the Ferry Between Faial and Pico	66
Ave de Nossa Senhora	67
Autumn	68
Fundamental	69
Araneus diadematus on Our Window	70
Murmuration	71
My First Poetry Mentor	72
Near the Nancy A. Messinger Trail at the Martin Wildlife Refuge	73
The Strategist	74
Skiing with Grandpa	76
Buttermilk Mountain	77

Someone's Truth

Not Everything Gets Lost	81
Cleopatra's Needle with Oranges	82
Cinquains: Bits of Stained Glass	84
Haiku for the Azores	86
Used-to-Be's	87
The Appointment	88
7 Largo da Matriz, Horta, Faial, Açores	90
16 Rua do Brum	91
Genesis 28: 10-17	92
Who Knows One?	93
Consul-General of Bordeaux, 1940	94
Wind Sock Nam	96
Flight After Flight	97
Disquiet	98
Benediction	99
Bridge	100
Uncover-up	101
The State of the Union	102

Acknowledgments 105
Also by Ada Jill Schneider 107
About the Author 109

PART I

Reliance

Reliance

I shudder to consider
the absence of you.
What would I do
without
the bread and butter of you?
Without
our dance of reliance,
its science and flutter,
without
my balance ruddered
by the essence of you?

I Fit Into His Arms

I fit into his arms
like a puzzle piece

drawn to him
like a magnet

run to the door
at the sound of his car

stand behind his chair
kiss the back

of his neck
so naturally

so lucky
tell me again

what exactly
does forever mean

I Scan Him Slowly

the way people scroll
down newspaper columns
for Unclaimed Funds.

He is my fund
and I have claimed him
but I scan him slowly
in case I lose him.

I can't take him with me
so I scan him slowly,
absorb him slowly
like the green ink blotter

I used in 5th grade
with my scratchy nib pen
at P.S. 184 in Brooklyn.

He was 6th grade
Captain of the Safety Guards.
He scanned me slowly
and claimed me fully.

Hardly calmly,
I scan him slowly.

Spring, 1953

(after Wordsworth and Paley)

My heart leaps up when I behold
the two of us on a bench
at the Brooklyn Botanical Gardens.
Me sitting on your lap amid
a crowd of Wordworth's daffodils.

A spectacle of golden daffodils
I never expected to see outside of
my senior year poetry anthology.
Yet there we were, a 10¢ subway fare
and seven stops away on the IRT.

Miles of dreams away from the tiny
bedroom where I did my homework
after everyone shut off the new TV
and went to sleep.

I breathed in that gentle day
to behold forever, along with rainbows
I stored in essays my English teacher
said were full of clichés.

But Wordsworth had it right.
Through the years, when I summon up
those days of rainbows and daffodils,
my eyes smile, my ears laugh,
and my heart with pleasure fills.

August, 1958

Two sultry nights and three sweltering days in Havana.
The floor show at the Copacabana. And us filming
every sight, no sound, nonstop, with an 8mm camera.
Your high school Spanish with the *piña* vendor.
The *Hotel Nacional.* Splashing my face with water
at the grand fountain. The architectural splendor.
All this during Fidel's cabal. We had no idea. Remember?

A Spoon and Fork

There is no denying
that a spoon and fork
make a good pair,
although sometimes,
one is more useful
than the other. In fact,
one cannot eat soup
with a fork; nor can
one pierce meat with
a spoon. Both
do pick up pieces.

The roundness
of the spoon is admired
by the slimness
of the fork, whose tines
are, in turn, appreciated
by the spoon.

Yet sometimes a spoon
doesn't care to spoon,
when all a fork ever
wants to do, it seems,
is fork.

All That I Am

I purchased a sheer, leopard print underwire bra,
matching silk panties, and half-slip about 30 years ago,
maybe more, and kept them wrapped in baby- pink
tissue, sealed with an iridescent-red heart sticker I had
to remove ever-so-carefully in order to touch them.

I must have bought them after dieting,
when I liked the way I looked, with the thought
of parading in front of my husband.

I stored them in the undies drawer of my traditional
18th century dresser, so far back, I was frightened
of pinching my fingers when I reached in to caress
the silk every now and then. After a while, they were
consigned to the moth-balled basement closet.

But on my husband's 50th birthday, I used my leopard
print underwire bra, matching panties, and half-slip,
along with several perfumed, promissory love notes
in between, to create a path up the stairs in order to
entice him into the bedroom for a gift of his choice.

Then there was the time I purchased a pair of black lace
stockings that went halfway up my thigh, exposing
the soft, white flesh above. I must have bought them
after dieting, when I liked the way I looked,
with the thought of parading in front of my husband.

I never did wear those stockings; in fact I returned
them. Nor did I ever put on the sheer, leopard print
underwire bra, matching panties and half-slip.
Like the leopard, I guess I just can't change my spots.

Happy 77th Birthday, My Love

If you lived seven hundred more years,
I would hit the jackpot.
The Milky Way would flash and dazzle
like a billion brilliant Jupiters.
The Aurora Borealis would startle and flare
then linger for nearly a year, as if God
had pressed some celestial sostenuto pedal.
Fireflies would think it August and flit their dance
in and out of the beach roses so you and I could point
and think how lucky we are.

Continuum

She smiles at him
with a familiarness
they call their own.
Little crinkles,
like diamond sparkles,
highlight their eyes.
A fifty-year continuum
of 8 millimeter frames
runs in the background
of their bones. *Now*
flicks to *then*
and back again
with the quickness
of an optician's hand:
"Is it one or two?
Two or one?"
Now or *then*?
Too close to tell.

Understanding

Sometimes we speak to each other
in dangling participles.

I know what I'm saying
and you know what you're saying

but what we are doing, however,
is trying to say what we're saying

so over and over, again and again,
we try to modify our words

until we understand one another
or, dammit, leave each other dangling.

Elasticity

I am your bungee woman
head over heels,
bounce to rebound,
always attached,
free-fall and all.
Between us
a certain elasticity,
a bouncing back,
give and take,
pliant pitch,
resilient catch,
back and forth
at your touch
like a swinging
weight on a string.
I always come back.

Graffiti Me

To prove
you love me
graffiti me
legally.
Spray-paint
MY NAME
in every font
on every wall
in front
of everyone
from here
to Verona.

Another Life

I always thought I'd love to be a dancer
if I had another chance at life. But here I am,
right now at seventy-eight, ballroom dancing
with my husband every Tuesday afternoon—
learning new steps, listening for the beat.

We laugh a lot when we Lindy Hop, count
the count while we waltz. When we dance
the slow and sultry rhumba, I look straight
into his eyes and see the years melt away.

His eyes and mine looking into each other
for nearly sixty years with sensations
that have pulsed through millions of synapses,
reaching back to the origin of melody
right through our own turns, our own toes.

A Slow Lindy

A slow lindy
is what I like best.
The deliberate beat
gives us time to meet
eye to eye
smile to smile,
come apart,
together again,
kick to the side,
in-between.

I go
under your arm,
so do you.
Together, apart.
You push me away,
bring me back
like
a familiar argument
about a dance step
and all that jazz.

Tango

Your arms take me where you go.
Your eyes make me go where you go.
Deliberately slow, slow, quick, quick, slow.

Your hand on my waist—a cue to swirl.
Back, turn, I dramatically whirl.
A stalking staccato—a slithery swirl.

When you draw me to your chest for a corté,
your thigh between mine when we corté,
you lead. I do not resist. I obey.

A little world on a compass rose.
Slow, slow, tango close.

Waltz

I want to write a poem about a waltz
that glides across the page in one long stride,
then pivots. I want it to *loop turn* in time,

move forward three lines, back, forward two more.
I want every single *triple twinkle* to rhyme
with anise, pure white or raw unrefined

cubes of sugar in rimmed crystal bowls:
vignettes of three, sterling tongs in each.
Every *he goes-she goes, reverse turn* and *spin*

will be a whirling blur of spangle and shimmer.
I'll have this poem *mit Schlag*,*
swirling around till I am dizzy with you.

with whipped cream

My Limbic Brain *

My limbic brain
taught my iambic heart
to dance to the past
to go with the flow
to romance
what I know
to 1, 2, 3 on my toes
to hold close
and let myself go
where his hand
says to go
the two of us so
in tune in time
oh yeah
moon June
you got it
we got it
woo my heart
my limbic brain
make it start
again again
let it play
let it play
oh let it play

the emotional center of the brain

Sir Christopher Wren's Garden

We ambled into the shaded garden
of Sir Christopher Wren's home in London.
Hedges enclosed three sides of the garden;
wide wooden benches ran along each.
Performing in a corner of the garden
was the Aspidistra String Quartet.
Upon hearing their music in the garden,
we gasped and grasped each other's hand.
For the first time, in that garden near the Globe,
we listened to Shostakovich's "Romance" live:
our favorite piece of music, *our song*,
in Sir Christopher Wren's garden in London!
We made love in front of everyone.

Pas de Deux

1.
When our cruise ship docked in St. Lucia
and most passengers disembarked for local tours,
we sneaked into the Colony Club on Deck Six.
With an iPod in my pocket and tiny speakers in his,
we planned to make the vast ballroom our own.
Turned out we were not alone. Marthe from Quebec
was at the grand piano, playing tangos, waltzes,
rhumbas, one after the other, then another. We danced
to her music in workout clothes and sneakers,
in uninhibited euphoria, until we fell exhausted
into lounge chairs. The mirror ball trophy was ours.

2.
Color coordinated gowns slit up to their thighs.
A trio of beautiful Ukrainian women
in the Centrum, from 3 to 4pm, on piano, viola, violin.
Only a bartender there and us
and then that tango from "Scent of a Woman."
We danced. No one was looking.

3.
Once you hear "The Lambada"
you cannot get it out of your head.
You want to join Kaoma on the beach,
laugh and thrust along with the others, follow
the Latin beat of their line to the end of music.
So, even though we didn't know the steps,
we couldn't just sit there when the band played
"The Lambada" on the last night of our cruise.
We looked at each other, laughed, stood up
pelvis to pelvis, as if we were in Kaoma's throng
and shook our buns like nobody's business.

Cruise

Cobalt blue water,
rhythmic whitecaps

evolving to foam.

Ominous clouds
grey the sun.

Fathoms below
a sudden turn.

Swells rock the boat;
wind creaks its bones.

Doors open
and doors close.

A muffled sloshing.

Curled in our berths,
we wait for something.

Optional Tours for Married Couples

The point of helmet diving in Bermuda is that no lessons
are required, not even swimming ability, just a bathing suit.

At the coral reef two miles offshore, step by tentative step,
I descend ten feet down the ship's ladder to the ocean floor.
              Schools of jeweled bream—translucent
      with a single purple dot—and sergeant majors—
                five vertical stripes on their sides—
dart in and out of waving sea fans and pink coral.

Suddenly, I realize that despite the heavy diving helmet
on my shoulders, I cannot grip the seabed with my toes.

I fear I am going to fall flat on my face in this fluid world,
the ocean filling my helmet till I drown.

Bobbing about in throes of tachycardia, I want out.
My husband's eyes catch mine, helmet to helmet.

He reaches out for my hand and I grab on for dear life.
I think of God extending His hand to Adam on the ceiling

of the Sistine Chapel, and us sitting on a narrow bench beneath,
comparing Fodor guide book photos with the real thing.

PART II

Working Class

Working Class

Why does working class run through my marrow?
My father's lunchbox, his union dues.
The steel beams he carried "for a better tomorrow."
Why does working class run through my marrow?
Dad was the laborer, his boss like a pharaoh
whose coffers Dad filled. He hauled like a mule.
Why does working class run through my marrow?
My father's rough hands, his carpenter tools.

Privilege

Chaos in the universe? Fate? Serendipity?
Why wasn't I born into sumptuous royalty?
To live in a veritable museum brimming
with intricate privileges of responsibility?
Where dust motes stream through stained
glass windows, and the past echoes off
terrazzo tile in expansive baronial halls.

Among the metal suits of armor, I would
line up my little brother Sid's lead soldiers,
and showcase his confident, knee-scuffed
baseball uniform, his *Louisville Slugger*,
and mint 1948 Stan Musial Rookie Card.

An elaborate ancestral oil portrait of *Dad the Foreman*, self-assured in his carpenter's
overalls, would be framed in baroque gilt.
A small, dated brass plaque would explain
that on this extraordinary day he received
a $2 tip and treated us to ice cream cones.

Next to it, a magnificent silk, hand-woven,
15th century-type tapestry triptych of *Mom, the Lady of the House*: on the left, in front
of the kerosene stove, stirring crepe batter;
center, wearing a Stone Marten fur draped
around her shoulders; on the right, posing
in front of her new GE washing machine.

As for me, my future might have been history,
my name and title on illuminated scrolls.
Yet, who knows? Cherubim, looking down
from hand-painted heavenly ceilings,
might find me resenting my monogrammed
life and trying to daydream my way out.

Brooklyn, 1941

When Shimmie lumbered down the street with palsied
                                                                 gait
in the 1940s, everyone in the neighborhood stared
at him. Mama, who was deaf, would always appeal
to us to be kind. "He can't help being that way
any more than I can. Show a little mercy."
We acknowledged Shimmie with a smile and wave.

He responded with his contorted smile and wave.
We walked on, grateful for our normal gait,
wishing people would show Mama a little mercy,
make some attempt to chat with her, not steer
clear of her because conversing was way
too much trouble. We overheard Mama appeal

to God for help and solace, as she peeled
potatoes, sliced stinging onions, and waved
away her tears. Working in the kitchen was her way
of avoiding people—closing some mental gate—
shutting out the denigrating, curious stares
of a time when disabilities drew little mercy.

In my Brooklyn most working men, at the mercy
of their bosses, were hesitant to appeal
for a raise in pay. They knew they'd be stared
down or worse, lose their jobs—waved
off like houseflies. Unaware of the military gait
that lay in their future, they focused on a way

to put bread on the table, their only way
of holding on to a shred of dignity. At the mercy
of our high and mighty landlord (Oh, his jaunty gait!)
coming to collect the rent, we would appeal
for the promised paint job, and again, be waved
off with a "We'll see, maybe next month." We stared

at his back as he headed down the groaning stairs.
One lucky family saved enough to find their way
out of the tenements and buy a small house. Flags waved
red, white and blue from every stoop. Now at the mercy
of war, thousands of young men answered the appeal
for volunteers as munitions plants opened their gates.

We stared stunned, saluted our flag and prayed for mercy.
We appealed to God to find a way to save our brave boys.
Shimmie was waived from serving because of his palsied
                                                    gait.

A Familiar Song

Swaying in slow motion or rewinding
the old words in your mind? Which
comes first when you hear a familiar song?

Maybe the one you remember
hearing over the radio in 1943
when air-raid sirens screamed *black-out night*
and Mama pulled every window shade
tight-to-the-sill and shut off every light.

There'll be bluebirds over
the white cliffs of Dover.
Tomorrow, just you wait and see.

Did you listen for Messerschmitts to fly over
as you hid under your chenille bedcover?
Did you pray for the war to be over?
When Mama turned the lights back on,
was the war over?

Mama Greenhorn

The youngest of four sisters,
Mama was the only one
who could read and write English.

She had the faintest trace
of a Polish accent people mistook
for French. This delighted her.

Remnants of Polish were reserved
for insults and curses. Mama was
a master of sharp retorts.

What caught her up short was
Dad's piercing taunt: Greenhorn.
She had no comeback.

Mama abided Dad's mocking abuse
for years but when the government
introduced Permanent Resident Cards

to be filed annually by foreigners,
she felt publicly humiliated.
At the age of forty, she became

a naturalized citizen and voted
for America's hero:
General Dwight D. Eisenhower.

Leah

Mama was as insecure as her namesake
but any deceit, I suspect, was hers.
Cajoling my reticent father into marriage,
she was sure she could change him.
He doesn't drink. He doesn't gamble.
He doesn't run around with women
and I should be content with that,
was duly recorded in her soulful head
while her heart bargained for passion.
Sobbing into a crumpled remnant
of her own beloved mother's dress,
Mama appealed to God on a regular basis.
Though she recognized her children's praise,
what she yearned for was the *Song of Songs*.

How Not to Buy a Dog

A basket of Chihuahuas
and my mom is still looking
for Mr. Right. She needs love.
She will take her time. See
what the market has to offer.
Not rush into a relationship
like she once did, to escape
her older sister's carping.
Now she knows temperament,
the importance of affection.
She will choose wisely.
The Chihuahua who nuzzles
her leg, licks her hand,
whose eyes plead, *Love me*.
The prince she's been looking
for all her married life.

Best Wishes

white egret
and blue heron

at water's edge
heads bowed

like a bride and groom
at the altar

mulling last minute
pros and cons

rushing in on whitecaps
of the past

waning
at the shoreline

Plagued

for Jenny

Even if the government formally decreed
that, henceforth, his name and image be erased,
how do you forget him?

Even if you tore up every single old love letter,
donated every darned sock, shirt, and tennis sweater
to Goodwill,

or trashed his bottom-dented leather recliner
and deleted every damned sports channel
he ever signed for.

If you've cut his face out of family pictures,
someone will inevitably send you your old,
stained wedding menu

or smiling photographs of the two of you
at a party you went to, which they just happened
to come across

while they were clearing out or giving up too.
Even if you searched the corners of your heart
with a candle,

wooden spoon, and feather to get rid of every last
bit of him, he'd show up again
in your grandson's eyes across the *Seder* table.

Round and Round We Go

Should she have done more?
Could she have done more?
Would it have helped
and why couldn't they
and what about her?
She ought to get up
and would if she could
but she can and she should
but what if
she could have done more?

Survey

How would you answer this survey?
Would you do things differently
if you were given the opportunity
to reverse a past decision?

Could you have done things differently?
Were you obliged by tradition
to reverse an intuitive decision?
Did it alter the course of your life?

Were you obliged by tradition
to conform to the norms of the time?
If you altered the course of your life,
did you settle for less than the stars?

If you conformed to norms of the time,
did you please everyone but yourself?
Did you settle for less than the stars
and did you try to make the best of it?

Do you please everyone but yourself
and live through your children's dreams?
Are you trying to make the best of it?
Do you feel it's too late for you now?

Do you live through your children's dreams?
Have you given them every opportunity?
Do you ever feel it isn't too late?
How would you answer this survey?

Disorder

We light the candles and give thanks to God
for allowing us to reach this day.
My son teases my daughter, getting even
with her taunts of over forty years ago.
The grandchildren empty their Plague Bags
even before we explain the *Seder* plate
and say *Kiddush* for the first cup of wine.
Frogs suddenly appear, trembling
the wine glasses, almost tumbling them
onto my white Passover table cloth.
All come to attention as my husband breaks
the middle matzah and it isn't long before
the little ones are whispering plans to hide it.

Hungrier than Nachshon by now, we diligently
build our *charoset* and *moror* sandwiches
until my husband and daughter begin to gasp
and tear up from the hefty portions of *moror*
they have spread on their pieces of matzah.
They will never do that again; nor will I
ever distribute the Plague Bags early.
Some might shudder at such goings on,
but I was happy to have our family together,
pleased that the grandchildren have heard
the story of *Exodus* many times and look
forward to it, which is exactly what we desire
and for which we give thanks to the Almighty.

Hands Under the Table

It began with the iPod—
plugging our ears with buds
shutting out the world.
That ubiquitous dangling white
V connecting pocket to ear
from Hip-Hop to Mozart—
your choice, your little world,
your stereophonic aloneness.
On the couch, my husband taps
his iPad; my Kindle and I hold
hands. Thank God for TV,
a communal activity. We head
to our respective computers.
Hands under the table once meant
his fingers climbing up my thigh.
Now texting delivers the thrills,
hands sliding for messages.
A cursory glance to acknowledge
a dinner partner or group of friends
at the table, then heads down
in case someone has tweeted
within the last 15 seconds.
No one interrupts anyone.
All conversation takes place
under the table—like undeclared wages.
Reverting to first grade spelling,
thumbs work faster than tongues.
A retreat into little private worlds
in large public spaces.

*public: pertaining to, or affecting
a population or a community as a whole*
What have we become?

75 Holds on to Railings

75 holds on to railings
and is beginning to understand
that disappointment is part of life,
yet still hopes *not* for the proverbial best
but a happy-ending movie best
with everyone laughing and dancing in Technicolor.

75 is still a soppy optimist
even though flower power wilted and withered—
crushed by J. Edgar H. and crashed by LSD;
even though our now is splashed
with raving politics and ranting newscasts.

75 is still an idiot optimist
because her 7-year-old granddaughter loves
her American Girl dolls, Emily and Molly,
who love their family and country;

because her 9-year-old granddaughter
is trying to publish "The Adventures
of Jeff the Bunny and Mac the Cat;"

because her 15-year-old granddaughter
has just read "Night" by Elie Wiesel;

because her 18-year-old grandson,
the historian, believes in God;

because her 29 and 31-year-old beauties
turn their realities into experience
with creativity and tolerance;

because 46 and 50, her son and daughter,
work like crazy to support and nurture not only
the above-mentioned, but their very own dreams.

Because how can 75 possibly tell all these people
she loves so much, that they might have to settle for less?
Better to believe in the reincarnation of dreams.

Ice Hockey

Early morning practice, freezing at the rink,
huddled together at the edge of our seats,
we loved our kids with every inch of our being.
Parents in sync, freezing at the rink.

Early morning coffee, standing at the sink.
Thirty-five years have gone by in a blink.
Our kids are the same age we were then:
those days of slap shots and tournaments.

Offsides, faceoffs, heart-screeching saves,
taping sticks, carpooling kids outgrowing skates.
The future was vast freezing at the rink
but the past goes fast standing at the sink.

Once

Once I was pastel,
but the years muddied me
the way crushed grapes
become vintage cabernet,
or wishes,
tempered by reality,
make every moment
fraught with poignancy.

I Saw It Coming

Lentigines:
    a pair of gloves
    I don't particularly love

Lentigines:
    the size of lima beans
    on my face

Lentigines:
    spots
    where veins connect the dots

Lentigines:
    sporadically
    spreading along my arms

Lentigines:
    elderly
    is what it means

Time-Lapse

Who needs time-lapse photography?

Not anyone nearing eighty
who is shriveling by the minute,

crumpled as the monthly Medicare
statement crushed in her fist.

Not anyone tired of being toted up
by prescriptions, covered or not.

Or by payments to health providers
and who got what, or not.

Not anyone considering what to leave
to each child, or not.

Or whether it pays to clean out the attic
or leave it to the children to do, or not.

Or what collection
to leave to the local museum, or not.

Not anyone who knows
no one anyhow, gives a damn

about what she is thinking, or not.

Inventory of Birds

Embroidered Guatemalan birds migrate across
our formal dining room table every evening.

Above the TV, a weathered taxidermal mallard
keeps an eye on the life-sized tin crow staring at

the faded Audubon bird chart Mom and I bought
for $13 dollars at an antique shop on Route 44.

Dad, the minimalist, loved our teak egret purchased
in Copenhagen when Marcy was only 18 months old.

Heading south on the windowsill in single formation
are ceramic goldfinches, blackbirds, and blue jays.

The reverse-glass painting of a mockingbird perches
on the shelf above the silk Chinese finch we found

in Hong Kong when Greg graduated from high school.
The cardinal and evening grosbeak are stained glass.

These collectibles bring me endless pleasure.
They never grow up and leave, nor grow old and die.

You Can't Get Back In

You can get out but you can't get back in
through the doors on the arc of your life.
Why spend time on what might have been?

No sooner we start, then too soon we begin
to end. Youth has a temporary shelf life.
Once you get out you can't get back in.

Sometimes you lose and sometimes you win.
Make changes, take chances throughout life.
Forget regret for what might have been.

Why sway to the strains of the past again
when you can dance on the edge of a knife?
Once you get out you can't get back in.
Don't spend time on what might have been.

Regrets?

If I made a list of us,
the pros and the cons,
the highs and the lows,
would I do it again?

What would I do?
The goods were so good,
I would take the bads too.
Would you?

Memory Manager

I am firing my memory manager
with her obsessive, obsolete
system of filing every single thing
in one bulging folder labeled GONE:

pressed prom flowers,
cards of congratulations,
our daughter's dress-up birthday parties,
Harriet & Walter, her two white mice,
ice hockey tournaments,
listening to our son's electric guitar,
thousands of Red-breasted Nuthatches
on our first Audubon trip to Block Island,
my parents still arguing
despite the fact that they have died,
my smile without rippling wrinkles,
lists of hints for dividing perennials,
notes on how to care for ailing parents.

What is GONE has made me what I am,
so how can it be GONE?
GONE means lost, done, goodbye.
Memories should say:
"See you later."
"I'll always be grateful."
"I remember you then."
"I'll remember you always."

I am firing my memory manager
and hiring myself to re-format my files.

Tea Leaves

Don't let anyone
tell your fortune
in tea leaves.

Dire predictions
will your worst
obsessions
into headlines.

Drink your tea
and make
your own future.

Advertisement

This is an advertisement for tea.
Tea halts moping in its tracks like a border agent.
Tea gets you by the authorities with a fake passport.
Tea welcomes your new identity.
Tea gives you four hours to be who you wish you were.
Tea sings so you can write.
Tea makes you fall in love with yourself.
Tea lets you believe in world peace.
Tea lets you do laundry, write, and feed the dog,
                                        all at the same time.
Isn't tea amazing?

PART III

The Silence of Fireflies

Avian Victoriana

Victorian terns looped along platters,
weaving strands of cerulean satin
through vermilion roses and strawberry baskets
in gaily-painted profusion.

Peacock feathers and silver pheasants,
majolica finches in elaborate patterns,
Victorian keepsakes exemplified status
in bric-a-brac effusion.

Brimmed hats of feathered assemblage
trimmed from egrets shot for plumage
adorned women of Victorian vintage
in high-society fashion.

Victorian naturalists trapped or netted
specimens of birds for museum collections
exhibited in animated perfection,
a taxidermy illusion.

Spectrum

the intermittent illumination
of a 4th of July night—

the flamboyance of fireworks
exploding the sky

the silence of fireflies
sparking the air

flash and flicker
brashness and restraint

Tokyo man and Kyoto woman

In the Beginning

In the beginning
all was blank,
a clean slate,
an open book.

Then out of the firmament—
a belted kingfisher,
blue and grey as the waters
of the Taunton.

His plumage—
anointed with oil.
His crest—a crown.
His white-banded breast—

a banner of proclamation.
He knows what I don't:
he will return again and again.
I hover above

my new bird journal,
enter his name,
the date, the place.
My bird world begins.

Seven Little Goslings

Buoyant on the river,
two Canada Geese
bookend their downy babies:
seven little goslings.

Seven little goslings
who one day will mingle
with two hundred relatives
to feed, float, and poop
right in the middle
of our town reservoir.

Seven little goslings
who one day
will contaminate
our water supply,
but for now look as cute
as stuffed animals
on my granddaughter's bed.

Seven little goslings
who make me giggle,
who bring to life
my old picture books,
where babies always stay
babies with every probability
of future happiness,
even if they dig holes under
fences or lose their mittens.

Oh, let me stay giddy
with these seven little goslings
and never grow up.

Starring the River

In the morning,
when your home is on the Taunton,
you draw the drapes open
like a theatre curtain
for God's production of Day.

The sun's slow rising glow
in pastels across the sky,
a Greek chorus of Fall River hazy hills,
backdrop to the Taunton's tidal flow.

A buoy marks stage right,
a gull's raucous cry,
an unfurled sailboat lazing by.

Finches come to feed,
mourning doves beneath,
chickadees swoop in and away.

The sun begins to gleam and glint
off iridescent throats of mallards,
off gorges of our little hummers.

Someone turns on the sprinklers,
cable news, the coffee pot.

To Hold a Hummingbird

I went to Arizona
and remember
staring at the splendor
of nurture in miniature,

wishing I could hold,
in my cupped hand,
this little green, iridescent
needle-nosed thumbprint,

her nest, and two eggs
smaller than jellybeans,
altogether a fitting size
for a Japanese *netsuke*.

Hummers on Guard

Handsome in green uniforms,
their ruby-throated gorges glinting
like medals in the sun,
they fly hundreds of miles
searching for red booty
to claim for themselves,
never forging community.

They defend their territory,
hovering above it using scare
tactics, threatening to attack
one another with sharp,
little God-made swords.
Why these sugar-water wars?

The Azores in May

The blue hydrangeas
are not in bloom
so the *Ilha do Faial*
is not *azul*

but the *impérios*
of *Terceira*
are birthday cakes
with sugary roses
in pastel paint.

The grapes in *Pico*
grow upside down
sheltered by
black stone walls

and the regal cows
of *São Miguel*
pose all day long
on verdant hills.

The Sidewalks of Ponta Delgada

mosaic sidewalks
cobblestone carpets
paved like a painting

spirals and circles
octagonal stars
pineapples and corn

symmetrical curves
checkerboard boxes
geometric swirls

optical angles
triple loops of rope
double rows of chain

curlicue columns
sinuous lines
unending designs

pictures and patterns
basalt and limestone
handmade sonata
Ponta Delgada

On the Ferry Between Faial and Pico

the grandeur of volcanic rocks,
their black thrust through the blue expansive sea
like silhouettes of clipper ships
navigating the swells of history

Ave de Nossa Senhora

When Herod felt threatened
by the newborn king of the Jews,
an angel appeared to Joseph in a dream
and told him to flee to Egypt
with Mary and the child.
A little black and yellow wagtail,
Ave de Nossa Senhora,
followed behind
and swept away their footprints.

My Mom used to say that when we die
a little bird returns our souls to God.
So when I found a black and yellow
Goldfinch feather
the morning after we buried her,
it was a sign to me
that Mama was safe
and all was as it should be.

Autumn

Kingfisher flies in.
Hummers fly out.
Summer is gone.
Again.

Fundamental

Autumn
dismantles
summer
petal by petal.

Virile and fertile
slowly
grow fragile.

Araneus diadematus on Our Window

Carried by the wind on a filament of silk,
she was on her own the day she was born.
No mother, nor mentor to teach her,
this spectacular spider created a circular web
with remarkable rhythm.
Extrude, spin, tighten.
Extrude, spin, tighten.

She took center stage in her intricate orb,
a trapeze artist in yellow and white tights,
bearing what looked like a cross
on a coffee bean sack on her back.
No, on her abdomen.
Her crablike, soda straw legs hung
from silken threads. All of a sudden,
she reeled in her safety net and ate it!

Each day she spun her web anew
and put on her acrobatic show.
This morning she was gone.

Murmuration

In ominous formations,
every evening at rush hour,
speckled black starlings swarmed
the old Brightman Street Bridge.
Dark clouds of dread, I always thought.

But when I learned that a crowd
of starlings is called a *murmuration*,
my mind fluently changed direction
and maneuvered my perception
from menacing to mesmerizing.

My First Poetry Mentor

for Louis

The New England Yankee
upper-class-name-dropping side of him
rubbed up against his Agent-Orange-Vietnam-Vet parts.
A ratio of pain to girth.
Everything about him was expansive.
He knew people. He knew Boston.
He knew art dealers
and he named names of the unscrupulous.
His poetic pronouncements on social injustice
ran single-spaced, margin to margin.
No thirty-two-line poem
could contain all he needed to convey
about race or bureaucracy
or Helen Vendler's "favorites."
When Alice Quinn suggested he trim his poems,
he said, "She wouldn't recognize a good poem
if it stood on its head." And I believed him.
I believed every word he said.

Near the Nancy A. Messinger Trail
at the Martin Wildlife Refuge

At a distance, we presumed it was mother and foal.
The perfection of caring, the protection of giving.

But it was a white mare and a white donkey.
Grazing the same patch of grass tells you they are friends,

says my friend who knows these things.
They have worked something out between them.

My friend grew up as a New England barn girl who lived
for riding.
She has trained horses and dogs but opted out of having
children.

I was a New York City girl who rode trains and never had
a pet.
A family woman, I am devoted to my children and
grandchildren.

My friend is Protestant; I am Jewish. She swims the bay
and cycles marathons.
I garden and birdwatch. She can speak Chinese.
Me? Urdu.

Our differences fascinate us. Our writing unites us.
We can spend hours
contentedly grazing synonym finders for a perfect word
that means *satisfaction*.

The Strategist

for Christine

The hotel dining table was round,
yet she sat at its head.
At her side, her husband and son,
her friend George, and us.

Not her custom-tailored silk blouse,
nor her black cultured pearls,
rather her spirited countenance
drew our attention.

She plotted *her* strategy
for our next day of skiing
with the experienced confidence
of a Chief Operating Officer.

On the small Davos map,
her fingers *shussed* down *les pistes*,
raced to cafes she remembered
via lifts she knew by heart.

Per her usual efficiency,
the sun shone and snow glistened
with our wake-up calls.
The train arrived on schedule.

We followed with assurance
as she guided us down *les pistes*,
over moguls, through shade trees,
to Number 21—a thirteen-mile stretch.

Triumphant at the end of the trail,
our group congregated while
she took out her corporate iPhone,
snapped a photo, and emailed it.

Then she dialed the United States.
"Hi Daddy," she said. "Guess what?
I just skied the '21 Trail' for you.
I love you."

Skiing with Grandpa

A grandpa from Massachusetts
buckled his granddaughters' ski bootsetts.
They took tow ropes
up bunny slopes
in their brand new *Lands' End* snowsuitsetts.
After several seasons,
Grandpa saw no reasons
why they shouldn't try black diamond routesetts.

At Sunapee, Gunstock, and Loon,
they made "S" curves all afternoon.
Should one take a spill,
Grandpa was on the hill
to collect them and their stuff that was strewn.
Up and down chairlifts and lines,
the granddaughters' skills were refined
and it's way past their Grandpa they zoomed.

Now, they speed-race to a snow-spray standstill
and wait at the base of the hill
to look after him
as he looked after them
should Grandpa, God forbid, take a spill.
Not anymore
does he ski nine to four
but he's still going and skiing downhill.

Buttermilk Mountain

Alone,
alone
making "S" curves,
you want to spend miles of time
on the silent
white slope,
silent but
for the shush of your skis.

Is holiness optional
on this
man-made trail of packed snow
glissading
through
a dense forest of aspens protecting
both sides of you,
presenting
their tiny, heart-shaped leaves,
and above, the open blue sky
breathing in
warm little puffs of gratitude
wafting from
deep
inside your down vest?

PART IV

SOMEONE'S TRUTH

Not Everything Gets Lost

Not everything gets lost through time.
Bits and pieces of majesty, matter-of-fact brutality,
traces and puzzles of pottery are preserved.
Broken-nosed statuary, razed reliquaries, religious solutions,
colliding salvations are buttressed in stone.

Songs may be recaptured, languages deciphered,
generals remembered, profundities questioned.
Boundaries may be resurrected; historic layers
of rhetoric or fanatic declarations of morality revived.
Not everything gets lost through time.

Seeds of someone's truth steeped in arrogance
may transcend time, germinate in the name of honor.
Seeds of someone's truth spewed with vengeance
through centuries, contaminate in the name of glory.
Buried within ashes of the vanquished
        in restless fields,
                seeds of someone's truth lie.

Cleopatra's Needle with Oranges

Tapered and monolithic,
often embellished with hieroglyphics,
an obelisk is a four-sided pillar of stone.
Not erected alone,
but rather in pairs, they were found at the entrance
to ancient Egyptian temples.
FYI: In encyclopedias, the asterisk
next to *Egyptian Obelisks*
will refer
to the U.S. Naval Officer,
Henry Honychurch Gorringe
(whose name rhymes with orange).
He is the gentleman responsible
for moving the obelisk, AKA *Cleopatra's Needle*,
from Egypt to Central Park in NYC in 1881.
A formidable task it was, to move the 200-ton
red granite needle by ship across
the Mediterranean Sea, then the storm-tossed

Atlantic Ocean, to the Hudson River, and finally,
across a railway trestle specially
built, to where it now stands, not far
from the Metropolitan Museum of Art.
Over 1000 years old during Cleopatra's lifetime,
the needle's 68-foot-high twin is in London.
The two obelisks,
originally erected in Heliopolis,
were moved to Alexandria by the Romans,
and installed in the *Caesareum*,
a temple built by Cleopatra to honor Marc Antony.
Both obelisks were toppled eventually
but fortuitously fell face down, thus preserving
most of the hieroglyphics from weathering.
When Henry Honychurch Gorringe
(whose name rhymes with orange)
died, erected over his grave was a fitting mantle,
a miniature copy of *Cleopatra's Needle*.

Cinquains: Bits of Stained Glass

I walk
down the hallway,
to the stairwell, up the
staircase: beams of sunlight stream through
stained glass.

Dazzling:
metal oxides,
sand transformed by fire,
bring forth Favrile iridescent
stained glass.

Painter,
spectacular
glassmaker, vase maker:
L.C.Tiffany, master of
stained glass.

Disclosed:
Clara Driscoll,
hidden creative force
behind prized Tiffany lamps of
stained glass.

Turning
kaleidoscopes
fracture arcs of rainbow
into jeweled shards of tumbling
stained glass.

Prayer plants
fold their streaked leaves
at the feet of angels
etched in arched windows of antique
stained glass.

The space
between cusps in
ornamental Gothic
window tracery is graced with
stained glass.

In mosques,
churches, chapels
synagogues and temples,
we seek God through the beauty of
stained glass.

Zurich:
Chagall's vivid
thirty-foot tall windows
of biblical depictions in
stained glass.

Kaddish:
In the chapel
Twelve Tribes of Israel
comfort me in multicolored
stained glass.

Haiku for the Azores

caldeiras, islands
explosions over eons
mountains in the sea

hydrangea hedges
lush cultivated nature
cows in the pasture

baroque church façades
impérios of Faial
creations for God

inscribed in Hebrew
secluded cemeteries
Luso history

Used-to-Be's

The tour guide points out
some Jewish history:

on a doorpost,
the missing chink of stone
where a mezzuzah
used-to-be;

the first floor of
this three-story building
where a kosher butcher shop
used-to-be;

that contemporary library,
once summer home
to the Bensaude family;

the street
where Mimon Abohbot
used to live,
where the synagogue
used-to-be;

this entire port area
where the Jewish Quarter
used-to-be.

The Appointment

The very afternoon we landed in Horta, Faial,
Linda, Donna, Gil, Ron and I followed Bob out
of the Hotel Canal, turned left after four blocks,
took another left for six more to try and find:
*Eugenia Botelho (speaks English, knows about
a small Jewish cemetery in Faial). 2 pm at
The Regional Directory on Rua Consul Dabney.*

We found ourselves at The Ministry of Culture
where we were told that we had walked too far.
"The Regional Directory is two blocks back."
So Linda, Donna, Gil, Ron and I followed Bob
up a broad set of steps to an imposing building
with a tropical garden. A well-dressed gentleman
approached and informed us, in halting English,
 "No Eugenia. This historic house to Dabney
family. Now live Consul-General of Azores."

Determined to find that small Jewish cemetery,
Bob, Linda, Donna, Gil, Ron and I consulted
our hotel map and walked east until we spied
an open door to another official building, where
we got directions, in English, to "This Eugenia."
At the door of The Regional Directory, a fellow
told us, "Eugenia Botelho back in two hours."
When we went to wait at her office, we were told,
"This wrong Eugenia Botelho. Eugenia you want,
she come back at two o'clock."

A gilt-framed map of Fall River in the hallway
gave us hope. The right Eugenia Botelho (who
had gone home to breastfeed her baby) rushed in
at 2 pm, made a phone call, and suggested we meet
the town reference librarian. Asking for directions
in paltry Portuguese as well as in *un peu français,*
Bob, Linda, Donna, Gil, Ron and I finally found
the *biblioteca*, once home to the Bensaude family.

We mulled and mumbled while Bob conferred
at great length with the librarian about the key
to the Jewish cemetery. He offered to escort us
to the home of a woman who owned not only
this key but historic Azorean-Judaica as well.
So Bob, Linda, Donna, Gil, Ron and I followed
the librarian, single file, past shops, down narrow
cobbled streets to *7 Largo da Matriz*, to meet
Luna Benarus, the last link to Judaism in Faial.

7 Largo da Matriz, Horta, Faial, Açores

Historic 3 story home, built circa 1860, in center of commercial district, *Igreja Matriz* Plaza. Ground floor suitable for business, contains wide expanse of built-in shelves and drawers. Hallway leads to large room used as office/library. Shuttered windows open to incredible views of Atlantic Ocean.

Home to 3 generations of the Benarus family, notably Moses Benarus, a Jew and diplomat who hosted U.S. Pres. Theodore Roosevelt in 1907. Roosevelt's signed portrait may be viewed, along with Jewish artifacts, such as Hebrew prayer books and an eternal lamp fixture, presumably from a synagogue of that period. Present homeowners, practicing Catholics, are Prof. Luna Benarus and her husband, Manuel Brum.

16 Rua do Brum

The *Sahar Hassamain* Synagogue
fell into ruin like an abandoned garden
gone to seed. The roof leaked, floors
rotted, vermin lurked. Sacred artifacts
lay scattered, covered in dust.

One man had the heart and held the key
to help the building stand its ground.
By the grace of God, others were inspired
to preserve the legacy of Jewish families
who migrated from Morocco to the Azores
in the nineteenth century.

The sanctuary is now restored, vintage
Torahs returned. Above the elegant
Sephardic *bima*, the crystal chandelier
reflects Azorean-Jewish history.
A small museum will tell the world the story.

Genesis 28: 10-17

On his journey to Haran,
when the sun was set,
our ancestor Jacob
stopped for the night.

He rested his head
upon a stone and had a dream:
a vision of angels going up
and down a ladder
between heaven and earth,
and of God standing above.

He awoke in awe and said,
This is none other
than the house of God,
Beit El,
and this is the gate to heaven,
Sha'ar haShamayim.

We are in the house of God,
Temple Beth El,
speaking of the gate to heaven,
Sahar Hassamain.

We are in Fall River
thinking of Ponta Delgada,
of red velvet Torah covers,
and filigree crowns,
of *Espírito Santo* and common roots,
of those who came before us,
of what might have been,
and of what yet might be.

Who Knows One?

Who knows one?
I know one. Jorge Delmar,
the last Jew left standing
in all of the Azores. The one
who holds the key
to the Jewish cemetery
in Ponta Delgada, in São Miguel,
where there is one last plot
reserved for Jorge Delmar,
the one who keeps watch over
Sahar Hassamain, the one
remaining synagogue
in all of the Azores.

Who knows two?
I know two. The second row
in Sahar Hassamain where,
as a child, Jorge Delmar
sat next to his uncle.

Who knows three?
I know three. Three founding
members of *Sahar Hassamain:*
Abraham, Solomon, and Elias
Bensaude. All three buried
in the Jewish cemetery
in Ponta Delgada, in São Miguel,
where there is one last plot
reserved for Jorge Delmar,
for whom there is no one
left to say *Kaddish*.

Consul-General of Bordeaux, 1940

*As the Nazis overran Europe, the dictator Salazar ordered
his Consuls to stem the tide of refugees fleeing into Portugal.*

Aristides de Sousa Mendes:
the official *signature* required
to swarm like lemmings
through Spain to neutral Portugal the sea

Aristides de Sousa Mendes:
the imperative *signature* beseeched
by passport-clutching crowds
holding their water parching in place

Aristides de Sousa Mendes:
the *signature* of anguish
that stonewalled politics
and changed history

Aristides de Sousa Mendes:
the tinder of his *signature*
that inflamed protocol
and destroyed his career

Aristides de Sousa Mendes:
the *signature* of conscience
that stood with God against men
rather than with men against God

Aristides de Sousa Mendes:
the *signature* of salvation
that rescued 30,000 refugees
and all their descendants

Aristides de Sousa Mendes:
the *signature* engraved
on medals schools streets
on plaques and parks

in Cabanas de Viriato
Lisbon Israel Bordeaux
America Montreal Brazil:
Aristides de Sousa Mendes

Wind Sock Nam

Like currents move a windsock,
so he is propelled—a haunted, human cylinder
whose ballast is shrapnel.

Still receiving static
on the dial in his head—intermittent numbers
of unaccounted men.

He jostles through new cities,
anywhere but home—prowls the clubs on islands
with mind-crowds of his own.

Moving with the currents
keeps commitment in check—accumulates memories
to help him forget.

Flight After Flight

for Phil

So he sat on the sofa, staring.
Muttering. I sat with him.
Pills, pills, and more pills.
I brought him tea. I talked him up.
Nobody could help him.
They didn't help him.
Dreams were the worst.
Every damned night
he jumped out of that burning plane.
His chute never opened.
Every night he free-fell,
the flesh dripping off his ribs,
melting down his khakis,
his spit-shined boots,
like a wax candle
caught in the firing line of a fan.
Terror seared on his face,
night after night.
I clutched him so tight,
my fingernails made moons on his back.
We were soaked with sweat.
I talked him awake, flight after flight.
I lived through it.
I'm here, right?

Disquiet

every war is a banner war
meant to stave off future war
but there never is an end to war
never an end to war

people come and people go
who believe that peace
will come to pass
but that day never comes

children grow up with hope
but hope doesn't grow with them
it slows as children grow
it slows

children grow up with love
that grows as children grow
when its time to go they pass
they pass along their love

though love is passed along
peace doesn't come to pass
hope slows down and wars
don't end wars don't ever end

Benediction

And the Mountains Echoed

Leave the Afghanis in peace
that they may resume
their traditional tribal wars.
There are enough poppy fields in our world.

Let the women who sit in purdah
peek through slits in mud walls
made to fit rifle barrels.
Let them have many more sons
and continue to pray for their daughters.

May they all tread safely
through Russian minefields.
May they find scrap metal
from downed British planes
and blown-up American tanks.

And may their graffiti artists
continue to spray-paint Rumi
on bombed-out palace walls.

Bridge

Twist, Spin & Blame:
a gerrymandered game
of *them* versus *us*.

Nightly newscasts:
limited in vision,
anchored in assumption.

Wretched are the elected
who sneer and smear
from slogan-dense bastions.

This war is not civil. Both sides
should give a little. A bridge
without a middle cannot stand.

Uncover-up

To get it right.
Something very primitive
yet resolutely human—

Uncovering cover-ups
where legality and illegality
clash and overlap.

A persistent task, intense,
yet somehow sweet,
like finding art in science.

Not an easy fix—to catch
a glimpse of catlike swiftness
in a posed picture.

You didn't see it.
Or did you?

The State of the Union

I am as old as Social Security,
older than seamless nylons or penicillin.
My utopian schemes of youth, once pinned
to bulletin boards on clean-hankie school mornings,
have blown the way of political promises.
My star-spangled dreams of harmony and justice
have fizzled into sparks of reality,
sputtering in the distended national gap
between resentment and contempt.

In what state is our beloved union,
this constitutional paradigm
of checks and balances where drawn lines
now seem once and for all parallel
with no shining agenda or clear perspective
of ever meeting any time soon?
Everyone has an answer.
Everyone his own truth.
Why are you so sure of yours?

ACKNOWLEDGMENTS

Grateful acknowledgment is made to the following publications and online websites where some of these poems first appeared.

Bigger Than They Appear: Anthology of Very Short Poems, Contemporary Prayers and Poems, Creative Transformation, Evolving Doors, The Jewish Women's Literary Annual, The Literary Hatchet, The Living Poetry Project, Midstream, The Mom Egg, My Somerset, New Forest Nickers, Obsession: Sestinas in the Twenty-First Century, Poems for Grandma and Me, Saudades: The Jewish-Portuguese Connection, Quarters of the Mind, persimmontree.org, sayitatyourwedding.com.

"Cinquain #5" appeared on a car magnet. "Graffiti Me" and "Once" appeared on umbrellas. "Tea Leaves" appeared on a Zoltan fortune teller card.

"Flight After Flight" won the Eastern Seaboard Spring 2010 Poetry Contest at *persimmontree.org*.

"Consul-General of Bordeau, 1940" was written for the unveiling of the portrait of Aristides de Sousa Mendes by Debby Macy in the New Bedford Public Library.

I want to thank my husband, Ron, for always believing in me and always loving me. Many hugs of friendship and gratitude go to "The Write Intentions," my writing group of over twenty years: Nancy Abercrombie, Lee Glantz, and Nancy A. Messinger.

ALSO BY ADA JILL SCHNEIDER

Behind the Pictures I Hang
The Museum of My Mother
Fine Lines and Other Wrinkles
Saudades: The Jewish-Portuguese Connection
with Ronald Schneider, MD
My Somerset
Poems for Grandma and Me
Aviary
Quarters of the Mind
with Abercrombie, Glantz & Messinger

Bookshelves: A Tribute in Poetry,
Somerset Public Library Centennial (editor)
The Heart of Somerset:
A Bicentennial Celebration in Poetry (editor)

ABOUT THE AUTHOR

Ada Jill Schneider, an award-winning poet, directs "The Pleasure of Poetry," a program she founded, at the Somerset Public Library in Massachusetts. She reviews poetry books for *Midstream* magazine. Her work has appeared in numerous literary journals, anthologies, and online. Ada and her husband, Ron, a dermatologist, live on the Taunton River, a great site for bird-watching. On Sunday and Tuesday afternoons they go ballroom dancing.

www.ingramcontent.com/pod-product-compliance
Lightning Source LLC
Chambersburg PA
CBHW032140040426
42449CB00005B/326